CHRISTMAS FAVORITES

Solos and Band Arrangements
Correlated with Essential Elements Band Method

ARRANGED BY
MICHAEL SWEENEY

Welcome to Essential Elements Christmas Favorites! There are two versions of each holiday selection in this versatile book:
1. The SOLO version (with lyrics) appears on the left-hand page.
2. The FULL BAND arrangement appears on the right-hand page.

Use the optional accompaniment tape when playing solos for friends and family. Your director may also use the accompaniment tape in band rehearsals and concerts.

ISBN 978-0-7935-1757-2

HAL•LEONARD®
CORPORATION
7777 W. BLUEMOUND RD. P.O. BOX 13819 MILWAUKEE, WI 53213

JINGLE BELLS

Words and Music by J. PIERPONT
Arranged by MICHAEL SWEENEY

Solo

Introduction

Jin - gle Bells, Jin - gle Bells, Jin - gle all the way.

Oh what fun it is to ride in a one horse o - pen sleigh!

Jin - gle Bells, Jin - gle Bells, Jin - gle all the way.

Oh what fun it is to ride in a one horse o - pen sleigh!

Interlude

Oh what fun it is to ride in a one horse o - pen sleigh!

00862506

JINGLE BELLS

Words and Music by J. PIERPONT
Arranged by MICHAEL SWEENEY

Band Arrangemment

00862506

UP ON THE HOUSETOP

Arranged by MICHAEL SWEENEY

Solo

UP ON THE HOUSETOP

Band Arrangement

Arranged by MICHAEL SWEENEY

THE HANUKKAH SONG

Arranged by MICHAEL SWEENEY

Solo

THE HANUKKAH SONG

Band Arrangement

Arranged by MICHAEL SWEENEY

00862506

A HOLLY JOLLY CHRISTMAS

Music and Lyrics by JOHNNY MARKS
Arranged by MICHAEL SWEENEY

Solo

A HOLLY JOLLY CHRISTMAS

Band Arrangement

Music and Lyrics by JOHNNY MARKS
Arranged by MICHAEL SWEENEY

WE WISH YOU A MERRY CHRISTMAS

Solo

Arranged by MICHAEL SWEENEY

WE WISH YOU A MERRY CHRISTMAS

Band Arrangement

Arranged by MICHAEL SWEENEY

FROSTY THE SNOW MAN

Words and Music by STEVE NELSON and JACK ROLLINS
Arranged by MICHAEL SWEENEY

Solo

FROSTY THE SNOW MAN

Words and Music by STEVE NELSON and JACK ROLLINS

Arranged by MICHAEL SWEENEY

Band Arrangement

ROCKIN' AROUND THE CHRISTMAS TREE

Music and Lyrics by JOHNNY MARKS
Arranged by MICHAEL SWEENEY

Solo

ROCKIN' AROUND THE CHRISTMAS TREE

Music and Lyrics by JOHNNY MARKS
Arranged by MICHAEL SWEENEY

Band Arrangement

00862506

JINGLE-BELL ROCK

Words and Music by JOE BEAL and JIM BOOTHE
Arranged by MICHAEL SWEENEY

Solo

JINGLE-BELL ROCK

**Words and Music by JOE BEAL
and JIM BOOTHE**
Arranged by MICHAEL SWEENEY

Band Arrangement

RUDOLPH THE RED-NOSED REINDEER

Music and Lyrics by JOHNNY MARKS
Arranged by MICHAEL SWEENEY

Solo

Introduction - Moderately Slow

You know Dash-er and Danc-er and Pranc-er and Vix-en, Com-et and Cu-pid and

Don-ner and Blitz-en, but do you re-call the most fa-mous rein-deer of all.

11 Moderate Bossa

Ru-dolph, the red-nosed rein-deer had a ver-y shin-y nose, and if you ev-er

saw it, you would e-ven say it glows. **19** *f* All of the oth-er

rein-deer used to laugh and call him names, they nev-er let poor

27 *mf* Ru-dolph join in an-y rein-deer games. Then one fog-gy

Christ-mas Eve, San-ta came to say, "Ru-dolph, with your nose so bright,

35 *f* won't you guide my sleigh to-night?" Then how the rein-deer loved him

as they shout-ed out with glee: "Ru-dolph, the red-nosed rein-deer, you'll go down in his-to-

1.

2. ry!" you'll go down in his-to-ry!" _____

RUDOLPH THE RED-NOSED REINDEER

Music and Lyrics by JOHNNY MARKS
Arranged by MICHAEL SWEENEY

Band Arrangement

LET IT SNOW! Let It Snow! Let It Snow!

Words by SAMMY CAHN
Music by JULE STYNE
Arranged by MICHAEL SWEENEY

Solo

LET IT SNOW! LET IT SNOW! LET IT SNOW!

Words by SAMMY CAHN
Music by JULE STYNE
Arranged by MICHAEL SWEENEY

Band Arrangement

00862506

THE CHRISTMAS SONG

Music and Lyric by MEL TORME and ROBERT WELLS
Arranged by MICHAEL SWEENEY

Solo

Chest - nuts roast-ing on an o - pen fire, Jack Frost nip-ping at your

nose, Yule - tide carols be-ing sung by a choir and folks dressed up like Es - ki -

mos. Ev -'ry-bod - y knows a tur-key and some mis - tle - toe help to make the sea-son

bright. Ti - ny tots with their eyes all a - glow will find it hard to sleep to -

night. They know that San - ta's on his way; He's load-ed lots of toys and good-ies on his

sleigh. And ev -'ry moth-er's child __ is gon-na spy to see if reindeer real-ly know how to

fly. And so I'm of-fer-ing this sim - ple phrase to kids from one to nine-ty -

two. Al - tho' it's been said man - y times, man - y ways: "Mer -

ry

Christ - mas, Mer-ry Christ - mas, Mer-ry Christ - mas __ to you."

THE CHRISTMAS SONG

Music and Lyric by MEL TORME and ROBERT WELLS

Arranged by MICHAEL SWEENEY

Band Arrangement

00862506